The Ultimate Cricut Guide for Beginners

101 Tips, Tricks and Unique Project Ideas, a Step by Step Guide for Beginners, Includes Explore Air 2 and Design Space Guides for Beginners

By Jennifer Bell

Table of content

Introduction

I am happy you have a Cricut machine. And I would like to congratulate you for taking that bold step of getting one. Whatever use you have in mind; maybe you want to venture into the craft world, you want to make use of it in the office or in the school, you have just what you need.

Having said that, I am sure you're hungry for projects and experiments. You are eager to do something, and that is why I am here to help. What you have in your hand is a guide. Not just any guide but it's the only guide that you need which would open you to that Cricut world. First, we would talk about the basics. More of a *getting to know your machine* thing then we would talk about mind-blowing ideas and project which you can do immediately.

Open your mind and reach dip for that well of creativity in you!

Chapter 1. *What Is a Cricut Machine?*

The best way to define things is to make use of other things which are similar and easy to understand then add that distinguishing sentence. Having said that, the best way to describe a Cricut machine is that it is a machine that looks so much like a printer, but it is used for cutting. Simple right?

Picture a printer in your mind, something like a broad one but now think of it as a cutting device and not your regular printing machine, and you'll have a Cricut. It uses precise blades and different series (templates) of rollers to cut any object you can think of. Cool huh?

Contrary to what most people think. Cricuts are not used for scrapbooks alone. In fact, this is the idea they make us believe from day one, but it is not true. The Cricut has been around for years, and the only thing we know about the machine is that it is meant for scrapbook or scrapbookers.

I was once like you not until I was able to see a demo of the Cricut explore some years back. Then the Cricut explore had this large library of cut files, and you can also upload your own. It made use of this special software on your computer or tablet which would allow you to use over 100 different templates for drawing and engraving. The most basic thing we do then is to design your template or what you want to cut in the Cricut Design space software, attach the cutting mat, confirm the settings and we are definitely good to go.

The Cricut machines have not only transformed the world of crafting, but it has been able to add special values and aesthetic to any simple paperwork. It is important for us to know here that the Cricut machine has several other models which include the Expression,

Expression 2, Imagine, Gypsy, Cake Mini, Personal Cutter, Create, Crafts Edition and Martha Stewart.

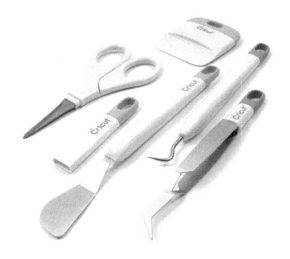

The Cricut machine is that tool that would definitely fit into any type of crafting you're involved in. And we shouldn't forget the die cutting machine which would give you that precise die cut that you need anytime. Cricut has allowed the process of cutting and crafting by hand to be reduced to its barest minimum and doing this would save you a lot of time. It would also make you move from one project to another easily. Furthermore, you can learn to work on multiple projects all at the same time, thanks to this machine. To improve accessibility, the Cricut machines are paired with hundreds of other themed Cricut cartridges. This allows you to change cartridges easily and would help bring out your creative side.

This bad boy machine would help you cut any material into that design you want. You can create that pattern on the design software that comes with it. This design software tool can come with a pre-loaded design that is ready for use instantly. You can make your unique designs, use an existing design and also update designs also. The cartridges also come loaded with so many designs that you can choose from.

You can buy these machines from an online store or at a craft store. And the price would definitely depend upon the model you choose. Furthermore, the prince can range anywhere from $100-$350 (and above), so it is better you narrow down your needs and go for it. Whatever makes your work more comfortable and efficient can be regarded as a significant investment.

The Cricut is one of them; it is rewarding and fun to use. Anyone can benefit from it. Because of its efficiency, we have Cricut in places we never envisioned that they would be in previous years. We have Cricut in offices and workshops. Does that sound strange to you? It shouldn't be because Cricut is never meant to be a home-only tool. It is time-saving and makes your work so professional, and the beautiful thing about it is that there are no limits to it, you can do whatever you can. If you're reading this book, then you have a Cricut machine in your possession, and maybe you don't really know how to use it. Well, I am here to help you with that.

Cricut machine has lineages. Yes, the Cricut you have now wasn't like that some few years back. But we shouldn't bother ourselves about the past but the future and little about the present.

First, we have the Cricut maker which is a machine used with design space. This Cricut maker has a cloud-based online software. And this particular series or design cannot function alone you would need to use the design space on a desktop or a laptop computing, and of course, internet connection is needed. Another special provision provided with the Cricut maker is that you can make use of the offline feature in the design space app whenever you're using the design app on an IOS device, i.e., an iPad/iPhone or MacBook. This means you can make designs and all without an internet connection. This is just one device, and that is not all because each device has its own peculiarities added to the general feature that we all know. We also have the Cricut Explore Air.

This invention of Robert Workman with the collaboration of fellow investors like Jonathan Johnson, Matt Strong, and Phil Beffrey is also pronounced as cricket. This product has been able to gather so many revenues in sales within a short period of time because of its effectiveness and handiness. Also known as Cricut expressions machine, the device electronically makes out shapes and images from paper, cardboard and other materials. Instead of you to make use of scissors or blade a Cricut is the easiest option. Robert didn't know anything about electronics; he just knew what his customers wanted. *I didn't know anything about electronics. I just knew what my customers wanted. A machine to electronically cut shapes.* This device which has been able to amass a 30 billion dollars annual sales and a four-year compound growth rate of 2.6 percent over a period of just four years.

This machine has been in work for years, and it totally blows everyone's mind and any other cutting machine out there. They keep bringing more and more to the table, and they keep adding something new every now and then. The Cricut has been able to dominate that market because of its reliability, performance, durability and its firmware also. This force of paper crafting revolution can also work without being connected or hooked to a computer. There are some designs that are portable and convenient to carry. Are you thinking of creating an endless assortment of shapes, letters, and phrases? Don't think too far, just get a Cricut.

The machine has gotten the scrapbooking community crazy because it has taken scrapbooking to another new level. In fact, the reviews from the buyers are amazing and even if you can't use it up to its full potential the little you can do now must have been able to wow you for long that is why you're reading this, to know more and do more. Cuts are made from the range of 1" – 5.5" high and up to 11.5" long. There are several cartridges provided for you to expand your cutting preferences and other measure dials which allows the utilization of different types of papers, cards, and other materials.

You might be thinking of going bigger. The Cricut maker is the latest addition to the Cricut cutting system. However, the Cricut explore air is also doing fine and is quite popular among users. We also have the Cricut Expression 24" Personal Electronic Cutter. There are two cutting mats of the measurement; 12" × 24" and 12" × 12" which also accept for cut character ranging from 0.25" up to a very impressive 23.5" Furthermore they allow for different languages, measurement, and several other settings. The Cricut Expression has a screen which shows you what you are typing or what you are working on. It is an LCD screen so you'll surely enjoy the display. The screen makes it good for the classroom and home business also.

The Cricut create blends portability of the first machine perfectly with the functionality of the Cricut Expression machine. The Cricut Create is this smaller machine which can only allow 0.25" cuts to 11.5" while it is on a 6" by 12" cutting mat. You have several modes to bring out your finished work, and this doesn't only work for the Cricut create but for all Cricut machines too. You can decide to Fit Page mode (this include selecting the largest size possible), Portrait mode (for taller pictures) Center Point function, Flip function, Auto Fill mode (used for mass production of cuts) and many more. Cricut machines come with different hardware designs. Some have the buttons and the display screen while some are touch-enabled and they are very sleek also. When you buy a Cricut machine you get; shape sets, cutting mats, cutting blades, storage

tote, and paper-shaping tools, so you have the complete kit for all your needs.

You must have noticed that we keep saying *other materials, other materials* but I would like to state the kind of fabrics we can possibly cut. And yes, we can cut just about anything you want! The Cricut maker can cut materials that are up to 2.4mm thick, and it can cut some materials that are thin and delicate as tissue paper. There are over 100 plus materials the Cricut maker can cut. Some of them include; Adhesive cardstock, flat cardboard, flocked cardstock, flock paper, Kraft board, Kraft paper, construction paper, Dry Erase Vinyl, Holographic Vinyl, Metallic Vinyl, Metallic iron, Printable Iron, Wool Felt, Silk, Duct tape, Magnet Sheet, Soda Can, Shrink Plastic, Velvet, etc. I would create a full list of this in the subsequent chapter.

Now the question on your mind would be; what types of fabric can I cut and do I really need a backer? For a Cricut marker, you don't need a backer especially when you use the rotary blade. The previous models of the Cricut would allow you to cut fabric with that regular fine-point blade, but you would need to make it thick by placing something, cardboard preferably behind. That is cool, but I am very sure you wouldn't want to always place an interface behind every time, so a rotary blade is very much appreciated. More also, the fine-point blade which is a feature of the previous Cricut cutter would cut fabrics, but it wouldn't have those nice clean and crisp edges so the rotary blade would do a wonderful job.

The maker can cut any kind of fabric from the very delicate ones to the heavy denim, sailcloth or even burlap. It can also cut fabrics like the sequined fabrics, leather, fabric with glitter on it, faux fur and quilt batting also. You can place any fabric directly onto the FabricGrip mat and cut it yourself. If you are involved in a project that requires multiple fabric designs the Cricut maker can cut through three layers of fabric simultaneously. The software is also easy for you to learn and you can use the ready-to-make projects that you have there.

Why I am very sure you can use the software is because the Cricut Design space is very intuitive. You don't have to be tech-savvy before you're able to create a design. Furthermore, it also has a little walkthrough tutorial that would get you on the go as soon as you set up the machine. It would show you some basic designs from the design space. You can twist or modify these designs to sooth your purpose or project or you can make your own unique designs also. I believe this is something you can learn within a few minutes. However, there is step by step videos that would be of help, and I would also provide some step by step instructions and procedures in this book also. This procedure would guide you into making your very own first project.

Chapter 2. What Are the Uses Of A Cricut Machine?

Quickly, I would list what you can do with a Cricut machine;

- ❖ A leather cuff bracelet
- ❖ Paper gift boxes and tags also
- ❖ Vinyl quotes for coffee mugs
- ❖ Iron-on Vinyl for your T-shirts
- ❖ Greeting cards
- ❖ Monogrammed water bottles
- ❖ Customized tote bags
- ❖ Paper pennants for parties
- ❖ Coloring pages for children
- ❖ Paper flowers and paper bouquets
- ❖ Decals for model airplanes
- ❖ Felt Coasters
- ❖ Stencils for wood signs
- ❖ Scrapbook
- ❖ Part of your car (I saw someone cut part of his car because he couldn't find the spare in the junkyard.

Asking the question, "What are the uses of a Cricut machine?" is an open-ended question. The first answer I would probably give you is that you can use Cricut to *cut* anything.

Any device that can allow you to cut pieces of other objects is actively involved in the construction process of your project. You can draw with a Cricut machine. Drawing with a Cricut machine is fun for signs and cards also. Cricut machines have peculiar markers which can work with the machine. However, anything which can fit can work!

Apart from scrapbooks, the most popular use of a Cricut machine is to create homemade greeting cards. You must have walked into a store to buy a greeting card. It doesn't really matter the type, birthday, Christmas, Easter, Get well soon card or just a friendly card. If you have one, flip the card and check the price.

One greeting card could be $4.00 and above. Isn't that expensive for just a simple card? Besides, some of us just settle for the designs and the words written in it because we don't really *have any option*. Left to you, you would want the card to have a unique kind of design with the best colors of the recipient, you would also want an original poem of yours to be written.

Handmade greeting cards are the solution here, and you can use the Cricut machine to make them. You have many designs, you can pick yours, use that color you want and you can include your original words. And have you ever noticed that people appreciate handmade cards more? Yes, people do because they appreciate the effort you have been able to put into making that card.

Furthermore, you might be thinking of your own seasonal decoration. A Cricut machine can help with that. Any season or holiday decorations can be created with this machine. You can get more than enough scrapbooking supplies made from the very comfort of your home. Just think of dazzling Christmas trees, valentine hearts or that Halloween ghost you would want to make.

Whether we accept it or not we enjoy creativity. Everyone loves to be creative. A Cricut machine is a machine that would not only bring out the creative part in you but would help you develop quick crafts within minutes.

Having said that, we should not forget that there is something cool about creating your own wall lettering. Okay, you want to have a nursery at home, and you need to get the wall painted, and you also need letters.

There is no need for you to spend hours trying to carve letters with blades; there is no need to hire a muralist for your hand painting. You can do this easily yourself with the vinyl die cuts from the Cricut machine. It would look so professional and would cost you less.

What's more, is that you can make your own die cut stickers as well. A very fun way of making your own die cut sticker is by using the Cricut machine. The die cut stickers are wonderful gifts for young children. No matter how outdated you think, they are you would still see the beam of joy in the eyes of your child when you offer him or her a sticker. They love to stick them everywhere. You can also use Cricut machines to create fun and colorful posters for a school project or just for the fun of it. Stickers like these can be made into any shape you can think of, and it would save you a lot if you get them from the craft store.

You can also render wedding favors, and party favors too when you create tags, bags, boxes, and other party creations. These creations can come in any form like hats, gifts, bags, banners and even other creations which are definitely tailored to the theme and color of the party.

The Cricut machine would allow your imagination to go wild because you'll definitely be looking for new ways to make cool designs. Are you expecting a child soon? Do you need to create that scrapbook filled with life? You can make use of a Cricut machine also. You can start with pictures from the day they were born into this world, and you can keep adding photos as they grow older. When he or she grows old or is getting married, you have this perfect gift.

Scrapbooks are not just any gift they carry a lot of memories and object that carries memories carry emotions also. If you're thinking of any fabric work, you also have the Cricut machine here for you. The beautiful thing here is that the Cricut machine can cut all kinds of fabrics. Yes, you heard that right, all kinds of fabrics. You just need to have the right Cricut machine for use especially the Cricut marker. Are you interested in any light woodwork or metal work? The Cricut machine got you covered. Anything you can think of, just name it. The Cricut machine is the best multipurpose craft machine in the world.

The obvious use of the Cricut machine which you can even find it the name is to CUT. Having said that, there are several objects the Cricut machine can cut. I have been able to make mention of some of them in the previous chapter, but here I would like to classify these objects into different segments:

Cardstock and Paper

I should state that the original idea of the Cricut machine was to cut paper and cards. However, the makers of this machine have been able to improve and develop it just as we have different needs. There are several papers the Cricut machine can work on; some of them include:

- ❖ Copy Paper
- ❖ Adhesive Cardstock
- ❖ Cereal Box
- ❖ Flat Cardboard
- ❖ Flocked Paper

- ❖ Flocked Cardstock
- ❖ Notebook paper
- ❖ Foil embossed paper
- ❖ Freezer Paper
- ❖ Foil poster Board
- ❖ Glitter paper
- ❖ Glitter Cardstock
- ❖ Kraft paper
- ❖ Kraft Board
- ❖ Metallic Paper
- ❖ Metallic Cardstock
- ❖ Metallic Poster board
- ❖ Paper Grocery Bags
- ❖ Paper Board
- ❖ Photographs
- ❖ Photo Framing Mat
- ❖ Poster Board
- ❖ Rice Paper
- ❖ Wax Paper
- ❖ Watercolor Paper
- ❖ Solid Core Cardstock
- ❖ White Core Cardstock

The Vinyl is next on the list. Cricut machines can cut vinyl which are beautiful materials for making decals, stencils, graphics and beautiful signs also. The Cricut machine can cut through the following Vinyl materials:

- ❖ Chalkboard Vinyl
- ❖ Glitter Vinyl
- ❖ Dry Erase Vinyl
- ❖ Holographic Vinyl
- ❖ Metallic Vinyl
- ❖ Stencil Vinyl
- ❖ Printable Vinyl
- ❖ Matte Vinyl
- ❖ Adhesive Vinyl
- ❖ Glossy Vinyl

On this same list, we have fabrics and Textiles. And like every material we have mentioned above, the Cricut cuts fabrics in that wonderful way. There are Cricut machines which make use of the rotary blade. The following are materials made of fabrics which can be shaped by the Cricut machine:

- ❖ Canvas
- ❖ Denim
- ❖ Cotton Fabric
- ❖ Faux Leather
- ❖ Duck cloth
- ❖ Felt
- ❖ Linen
- ❖ Leather
- ❖ Flannel
- ❖ Burlap
- ❖ Polyester

- ❖ Metallic Leather
- ❖ Polyester
- ❖ Printable Fabrics
- ❖ Wool Felt
- ❖ Silk

We shouldn't forget the Iron On Vinyl. We call it the heat transfer vinyl and the Cricut has its provision for this material. Most times we use the Iron on vinyl to decorate a t-shirt, tote bags and any other kind of fabric items also:

- ❖ Printable Iron On
- ❖ Glossy Iron On
- ❖ Flocked Iron on
- ❖ Glitter Iron On
- ❖ Holographic Sparkle iron on
- ❖ Metallic iron on
- ❖ Neon Iron on
- ❖ Foil Iron on

Apart from paper and vinyl, there are other special materials that the Cricut can work on successfully. I have been able to put together this very long list. As you read through I am sure some ideas would jump at you, don't forget to put it down and try it out.

- ❖ Aluminum foil
- ❖ Adhesive foil

- Aluminum sheets
- Adhesive wood
- Birch Wood
- Corkboard
- Balsa Wood
- Craft Foam
- Corrugated Paper
- Embossable Foil
- Duct Tape
- Foil Acetate
- Magnet Sheets
- Glitter Foam
- Paint Chips
- Plastic Packaging
- Soda can
- Metallic Vellum
- Printable Sticker Paper
- Stencil material
- Temporary Tattoo paper
- Vellum
- Washi Tape
- Shrink Plastic
- Printable Magnet Sheets
- Wood Veneer
- Window Cling
- Wrapping Paper
- Wood Veneer

There is a special kind of Cricut machine. Known as the Cricut Maker which can cut materials that are up to 2.4mm thick and several other types of fabrics which the Cricut maker can work on. They include:

- ❖ Cashmere
- ❖ Jersey
- ❖ Fleece
- ❖ Chiffon
- ❖ Terry Cloth
- ❖ Tweed
- ❖ Muslin
- ❖ Velvet
- ❖ Jute
- ❖ Knits
- ❖ Moleskin and many others.

The Cricut machine can be used everywhere, and anywhere paper is found. Which means you can find this machine in schools, offices, craft shops, etc. Definitely, the Cricut machine can be used for school projects, card stock projects, iron-on projects, etc. Furthermore, you might want to make your own window clings maybe for the holidays, or you just feel like decorating. Whatever may be the reason, the Cricut can easily cut window cling material into different shapes that you like.

It would be careless of me if I fail to mention that the machine can also be used for faux leather projects. Yes, you might decide to create lovely jewelry items or beautiful fashion accessories with faux leather or even any type of leather, the Cricut machine is available to help you. Stencil wood projects can also be carried out by the Cricut machine. Stencil vinyl is a wonderful material which you can use to create several signs, shapes, etc. You can also work on the adhesive stencil and the stencil vinyl also joining it to the wood then finishing it with that wonderful paint. After the paint is dried, you can remove the stencil vinyl, and you'll have that beautiful imprint.

I made mention of school projects earlier. The Cricut machine is great for preschoolers. Not the preschoolers themselves but the instructors and teachers. More also, if you're involved in any print and cut projects, the Cricut machine and your printer are two things which you need. The Cricut would allow you to print photos or images out of your computer and then you'll be able to cut it to whatever size you desire.

The options are endless, from printable magnets to sticker papers you can make customized gifts, bags, etc. all from the comfort of your own home. In fact, the list of the materials which the Cricut can work on should be enough for you if you still want to know what the Cricut can be used for. The Cricut brings out that creative you, helps you to achieve whatever you have in mind within minutes and what we all like about it is that it is straightforward to use.

Chapter 3. *What Are The Supplies You Need To Make Use Of A Cricut*

For supplies you need, I have created that long list of material supplies under the previous chapter. Yes, they are materials that the Cricut can work on so that automatically qualifies them as supplies. However, we don't need all because we are at different levels of crafts. Besides, you have your own area of specialization, and I have mine. But we shouldn't forget the fact that there are some basic supplies you should have. These supplies are necessary, and you really can't enjoy your Cricut use without them.

The fascinating thing about getting a Cricut machine is thinking about projects you're going to work on and the supplies as well as materials that you need. First, I would start with the necessary cutting materials so if you skipped the list in the previous chapter because it is probably too long you can learn from this.

- ❖ Basic Vinyl: This is the best option for your indoor items that can't possibly get wet. You can use it for wall sayings and canvas also.
- ❖ Glitter Vinyl: It is the same as the basic vinyl but adds that glitter to it.
- ❖ Outdoor vinyl: These are wonderful materials for your car window decals and possibly anything that can get wet.
- ❖ Dry Erase Vinyl: This is wonderful for labeling.
- ❖ Holographic Vinyl: It is the basic vinyl with several other colors looking at you all depending from your viewing angle.
- ❖ Chalkboard Vinyl: This is also good for labeling but can also be used to make calendars also.
- ❖ Printable vinyl: This is a perfect sticker material.
- ❖ Stencil Vinyl: This is perfect for your hand painted signs or screen print shirts.

The adhesive foil which also shares some similarities with the vinyl but has that nice shimmer to it is also something that you'll need to get. Next is the transfer tape. If you are trying to get your vinyl from the back of your project, making use of the transfer tape is the best option because it has that firm grip and can also transfer vinyl with glitters.

We shouldn't forget the iron on materials. These are the materials which are always applied to shirts, pillows, hats and other materials. You can get the following:

- ❖ Iron-on Lite
- ❖ Glitter Iron
- ❖ Holographic Iron On
- ❖ Printable Iron On
- ❖ Foil Iron On

The materials I would be listing next are essential, and they are needed just like the way you need the ones I have mentioned above.

- ❖ Cardstock: This is a great number of cards, cardboards, making cards, gift tags, gift boxes, scrapbooking materials, etc.
- ❖ Felt: This is perfect for making finger puppets as well as dress ornaments. You might want to use them for mask and headbands also.

- ❖ Faux leather: Perfect for making jewelry, key chains, baby moccasins, and hair bows too.
- ❖ Window cling: This is needed for temporary window projects, designs. You could also use them for your fridge and other appliances that need decorating.

We have been able to cover the material needs what of tools, pens, mats, and other accessories. Normally, the Cricut machine comes with mats and other accessories, but you'll need more because they would only provide you that basic one. You'll need:

- ❖ Mats: These come in different sizes. You have the 12 by 12 and 12 by 24. There are other sizes, but these two are the major ones. It is good to have at least one of each size in your box of tools. The materials you're working on would determine the size of the mat that you need. However, you need to get at least one of the following;

- ✓ Light Grip mat: This is in color blue, and it is used majorly for papers and cardstock projects alone.
- ✓ Strong Grip mat: This is a purple color mat meant for poster boards, thick cardstock and several other thick materials which you'll definitely work on.
- ✓ Standard Grip: This color green mat is meant for vinyl and iron on alone.
- ✓ Fabric Grip: A color pick mat meant for fabrics alone.

❖ Pens: If you're a craft person, you should have loads of this already. If not, get some basic colors and more.

❖ Tools: There are several tools you need to have when getting a Cricut machine. Whether you are getting the Cricut to explore air or the Cricut maker, you'll need the following tools to make work easy.
  - ✓ Spatula: This is needed to help you get materials off the mat

✓ Scissors
✓ Tweezers: This would help you in weeding those intricate details.
✓ The scraper is needed when you want to transfer tape to the vinyl
✓ The weeder: this would help you to remove the excess vinyl from any angle. You can get all these tools all at once.

❖ Extras like bright pads, easy press, cuttlebug, etc. are not basically needed. However, it is important that you have the complete Cricut supplies and these extras are also part of them. The right pad, for example, would make weeding very easy especially if you plan to work in low light areas or if you want to use a lot of glitters you must have this with you. Next is the cuttlebug which is a die cutter machine (not necessary). The easy press follows, it is a portable, easy to use a heat press. It would be careless of us if we fail to mention the storage totes. The storage totes are good for keeping the machine supplies safe and properly organized. There are of different types; rolling storage tote, Machine tote, and shoulder bag.

Chapter 4. *Your Cricut Machine Space And Its Efficiency*

The best way to utilize your time in your Cricut small business (if you have one) or during your project is by creating that impressive workspace. When I first started using the Cricut machine, I noticed that during a project I would have to get up from my chair to retrieve a supply or something else, so I decided to fix my workspace because it lacked efficiency.

First, wherever you place the Cricut machine is your workspace. Like I have said, it is like a printer and you wouldn't be carrying your printer all about except if it is a very mobile Cricut machine. If you already have a workspace, you should improve its efficiency and if you don't these few tips stated in this chapter should get you started.

The first thing is that you should draw a map of your workspace. Drawing that map requires you to make that plan. Like people say; *if you fail to plan, you plan to fail*. Make sure you have a good plan for your workspace. Where would your table be? Cupboard and chair? The Cricut machine should be placed on a very large table and not a small one so that you can work while sitting at that table.

Next, if you already have a workspace and you're working on a project, draw a line every time you get up to get a supply showing your current position and the position of the material or supply you had to get. This would be helpful. Finally, you evaluate these lines and look at the ones you use frequently. Then you can move those supplies closer to you, or you can rearrange the furniture.

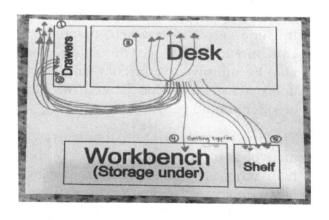

I wasn't able to draw an initial plan when I started using my Cricut, so I just positioned things the way I felt. So the drawing above depicts the state of my workspace before I made the necessary adjustment. Notice that I have so many arrows going to the drawers from the desk. That is because I store my craft supplies there (vinyl, paper, cards, and all other materials. I have a small chest of drawers where I do keep my new products. And the Cricut machine sits on top of it.

The craft space I have there is very tiny as you can see that the workbench is quite smaller than the desk. You might have seen that I drew some arrows facing the desk. Those arrows are depictions of the bucket I hang above my desk where I put little tools and supplies like blades, pen, markers, scissors, etc. I have a shelf beside the workbench. This bench houses all the Cricut machines I have.

After drawing that map, my eyes were opened to how inefficient the workspace has been and how I needed to change things also. First, I needed to place all the craft supplies into the craft room. I forgot to mention that the drawers weren't so close to the desk like it is in the picture.

They were in another room. Second, it is so much pain to walk around those drawers than walk back to use the machine then move to the desk again. So much walking just to get something done. Finally, I noticed that I didn't really need any workspace in my craft because I was only making use of that place as a storage unit.

What was I able to do to improve the workflow? First, I moved the workbench out of that position, and I turned the drawers. Plus, I added an extra shelf which was only meant for storing things. There is no need for a second map, but I would love to show you how I upgraded my efficiency with just some few changes. Check out that improved workflow below:

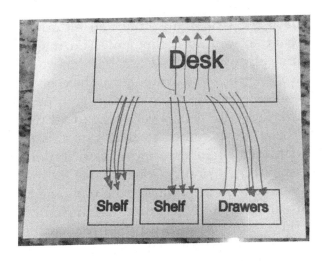

Better huh? So, I only make a journey to and from if I ever want to do something or work on a project. First, I don't waste time walking, and I have all I need within my reach. Now I would want you to sit down, draw out a plan. If you have a working space, you should work on how you can possibly improve it. Besides, this is just my personal workstation. It all depends on where you use the Cricut machine. If you are making use of it in a school or office, you are expected to create that craft station separately but still within your reach. Most schools have crafts room so pupils would do all craft in there. The crafts room would have the Cricut machine and all other tools as well as equipment. You might just place the Cricut machine on your work desk, and you get a box or a container where you can place your pen, scissors, etc. This is very easy to set up. There are two factors that you should consider when creating a workstation; Efficiency and Convenience. You definitely want to move from one project to another project without wasting much time, and you also want to reduce the amount of energy you have to put in to complete your project so that you don't end up having back pains

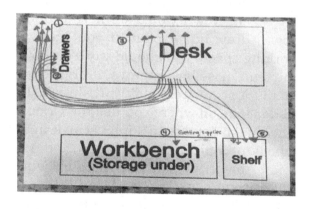

Chapter 5. *Maintenance Of The Cricut Machine*

This is an ultimate guide so it would be lackadaisical of us not to include care and maintenance of the Cricut machine. Even though the Cricut machines all come with guides and manual, I would like to pick the explore machine here because the manufactures would only give you the basic guidelines and instructions you are the one who would make use of it and would also condition it to what environment you decide.

You must have been able to go through the installation process, and you're probably using your Cricut already. However, over time and with consistent use your machine may have that deposit of dust or paper particles.

Furthermore, you may see some of the greases from your machine starting to build up upon the carriage track. This isn't good for the machine, and you would want to handle a Cricut machine in that condition because it also affects productivity. Cleaning the Cricut is very easy.

You can make use of the following tips when cleaning your explore machine:

- ❖ First, like every other electronic machine, always disconnect it from power before cleaning it. Your instincts should tell you that, however, we would still include it here.
- ❖ A perfect way to clean the machine is by making use of a glass cleaner sprayed on a very soft clean cloth.
- ❖ You may be faced with static electricity build up which causes dust or paper particles to pile up. Just wipe that part away with a clean cloth.
- ❖ There can be a buildup of grease on the bar where the carriage travels. What you should do here is to wipe that place with a clean cotton swab, tissue or a soft cloth gently.

It is also pivotal that you know the grease application Instructions.

- ❖ As usual, you should turn off the Cricut machine.

- ❖ Next, you move the cut smart carriage by gently pushing it to the left.
- ❖ Wipe the cut smart carriage bar with a tissue. You shouldn't forget to clean the entire bar also. If you don't know the carriage bar, it is the one the cut smart carriage slides on. That long thin bar just right in front of the belt.
- ❖ You can also move the cut smart carriage by gently pushing it to the right.
- ❖ For efficiency purpose, it is important that you repeat the process of cleaning the cut smart carriage bar with a tissue or a very soft cloth while you continue to wipe the entire bar.
- ❖ Gently move the cut smart carriage to that center of the Cricut machine.
- ❖ Open the lubrication packet with much care and squeeze a little amount of grease onto the end of your cotton swab.
- ❖ On either side of the Cut Smart carriage, you can add that light coating of grease which would be around the bar to make a ¼" ring on either side of the carriage.

❖ Gently move the cut smart carriage all the way to the left when you move it slowly to the right again. This would enable you to share the grease properly among the entire bar.

❖ Finally, you should wipe off any grease that would build up at the ends of the bar.

There are several do's and don'ts of the Cricut machine.

❖ Never should you clean the machine while it is still on. This may sound ridiculous but be sure that you unplug it before you start the cleaning process.

❖ Use a soft cloth always. A non-alcohol baby wipe is preferable. That is what I use.

❖ Be sure to clean out the blade housing to remove residues. It very necessary to keep this area clean and neat all times.

❖ Moving the hosting unit to one side to clean the case remains the best option.

❖ You should never spray clean your machine directly.

- ❖ Never wipe off the bar holding the housing. The grease you see there is meant to be there.
- ❖ You should never touch the gear chain present at the back of the unit (Explore Air)

If your explore machine begins to make that grinding noise you can ask for a grease packet to be sent to you. Well, this is meant for US/Canada only. Just contact the Cricut Member Care team. Lastly, there is every possibility that this product can irritate the skin or eyes. Therefore, you should keep it out of the reach of children and if there is any case of contact with skin or eyes you should seek immediate care by rinsing through with water and medical care if necessary. *It is a machine for God sake!* Yes, but all precautions need to be taken.

Chapter 6. *Explore Air 2*

The first thing you need to know here is that the Cricut air is a special type of Cricut series. Even though the most recent is the Cricut maker, the Cricut explore air is still getting much attention because it is still very effective and recent. The explore air 2 has the following: the machine, power cord, USB cord, Blade and Housing, Pen, Card stock samples, Welcome book and standard grip cutting mat just as it is shown below.

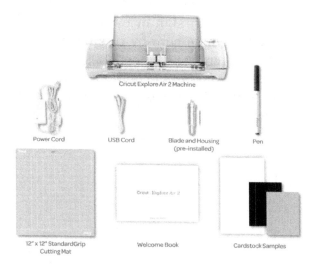

Cricut Explore Air 2 Machine

Power Cord USB Cord Blade and Housing Pen
(pre-installed)

12" x 12" StandardGrip Welcome Book Cardstock Samples
Cutting Mat

However, it is important to note that there might be variations in the boxes. This doesn't mean that you don't have the correct box; the components change with time. For your Explore Air 2, I would show you a quick diagram of all the parts. You can also get this from the welcome book.

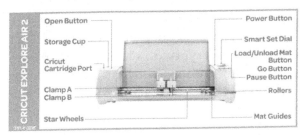

The Cricut explore one is that basic and economical machine that the Cricut gives us. Is it sold at $199 cheap huh? And because it is the basic machine it has all the precise cutting, writing and scoring expertise just like all the explore air machines. You can cut all the same materials. However, there are noticeable differences.

The first being that the Bluetooth isn't enabled like the Cricut 2. What this means is that you are required to run a cord from your device (computer/tablet) to your Cricut to connect both. This is no big deal, but it can be challenging especially if you want to consider your workspace. My first Cricut wasn't wireless, and I was still able to use it perfectly. Another is that you don't have a double tool cartridge.

What this means is that you can't write and cut or score and cut during the same processor in the same pass. This means that you don't have to do one before the other. You can still do your normal write and score; however, you would have to do it separately

Chapter 7. Design Space

The design space is not your workstation. But it is definitely part of your workstation. It is the space on your computer system, phone, tablet or whatever device you chose to make your design. It is that application where you can express your creativity. You log in on any device to your Cricut account, and you download it. And there is definitely an offline provision. If you're using a Cricut explore 2, it would be connected to your device via Bluetooth, and you can be able to print out just like a wireless printer. It has several features all depending on the version and your device. For the iOS version you can choose from over 50,000 images, fronts and projects also. You can definitely upload and clean up your own images, make designs without an internet connection making use of fonts and images you have been able to download on your device.

Furthermore, you'll be able to cut quickly and make those easy predesigned projects also. We shouldn't forget that if you are making use of a phone, you can use the built-in camera on your device to make that perfect position and you can also visualize those projects on the real-life background. The design space contains the design screen. There is a column by the left which has: insert images, upload images, add text, and add a canvas. The design space is just your workspace on your phone. How creative you are her would determine the outcome of your project.

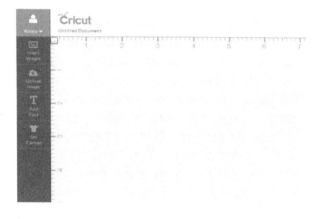

Notice the lines. You have to pay attention to measurements. You have different ways to create your project all on the design space. Working on the design space is divided into three: First, you arrange a design from scratch, next you select from the thousands that have been provided for you as *ready-to-make* projects then you tweak or modify it to your taste. What follows is cutting.

Just place your material on the mat, load the machine and you press the Go button. The machine automatically handles the rest. The final process requires you to assemble those pieces add, glue, sew or do anything you want until your final project is achieved. We wouldn't leave you in the dark here so the rest of this book would focus on projects that you can do on your own.

Chapter 8. *101 Tips, Tricks And Cricut Ideas*

So, we would start first with something very simple and easy. Most times when you want to celebrate the beginning of the year, we begin to take time to enjoy the memories of the previous year in the hope that the forthcoming year would be great. This is a simple project that you can use to *start* that new beginning. It is not a card, I know cards are so popular, and you'll probably think cards or scrapbooks would be the first on the list. It is a happiness jar! Sounds strange, well it is just to tell you that you are free to do whatever you want.

The idea is similar to New Year resolutions but distinct in the sense that this requires you to store up happy moments in a jar instead of making goals that you'll need to achieve. When you have this, it would be a tangible reminder of all the good things of your life. Making that happiness jar is quite easy. You just have to work on the cute decals which you'll be putting in the jar.

Items

❖ A jar large enough to hold 365 days' worth of happy memories.

❖ The self-adhesive vinyl in whatever color you choose.

❖ 65 lb. letter-size card stock. You'll be using 16 sheets to get 365 hearts. One for each day.

❖ Cricut for cutting the cardstock

❖ SVG files and patterns which are available in your free resource library.

Process

❖ Download patterns for the project from your free resource library. If you are using the Cricut which I know you would be your first option, you'll be required to upload the file to your design software.

❖ Next, you'll cut out the vinyl and apply it on your need clean jar. The design above allows 25 hearts on a sheet. You may want to cut 16 sheets to all that is required for 365 days.

❖ You use your marker or pen to write down something that made you very happy today on that heart-shaped paper. Anything. It may be just a face, a lyric from a song, a memory, that idea or something else. Fold it and put it in the jar. Repeat this process every day of the year. Simple huh?

We should explore all the materials while we still remain on that single level. The next project would be *putting vinyl on mugs plus cute designs.* How can you put cute face designs on your mug to make them look good like the ones below;

Even though this project is ridiculously easy, it might be tricky because not all mugs are meant to be decorated. So the first thing for you is to:

- ❖ Know the mugs that would work best. Especially those curved ones. You can always picture how it would be by just looking at the clean surface.
- ❖ Know the kind of Vinyl you can put on the mug so that its color would not peal. You'll be

thinking of a water-resistant Vinyl.

❖ Then you look for cute simple designs like cute kitty and puppy faces. I designed the one below

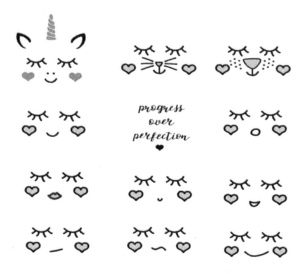

Items Needed

- ❖ Ceramic Mugs. Any item powdered coated or textured should be avoided.
- ❖ The outdoor permanent adhesive vinyl. I used the Oracle 651
- ❖ Next is the transfer sheet
- ❖ Scraper or card
- ❖ Cricut for cutting
- ❖ SVG/DXF/PDF cut files and patterns

Process

- ❖ You'll cut the cute designs out for the mugs.
- ❖ You're definitely going to use the Cricut machine, so you just upload your design file to the software. Cut it out and paste on the mug. Simple!

You can put the mug in the dishwater it is safe for now, but after a while, it wouldn't be as beautiful as it was. But you can always remake it, right?

The next idea is something very seasonal. However, you can use the method to do other things. It is a

Christmas Tea Towel. This is a project that can be completed perfectly with the Cricut machine. First, you must know how to use the easily customized pencil pouch on your software.

- ❖ You open your design space once again, and you get your images from the available library. This time you're involved in writing so you'll click on text. You pick the right fonts size and font style.

- ❖ I chose the hand-lettered "Merry Christmas" for this project. You can write whatever you want. What makes the explore air special is that it has that dial setting. This means that you wouldn't trouble yourself about changing the blade depth or trying to crack your head about the depth that matches up to each material. For this project, you'll make sure that you set the dial to "Iron-on."

- ❖ Then you would gently place your heat transfer vinyl on the cutting mat making sure that the shiny side is faced down. Load it into the machine and press the cut button but you should never forget to mirror the images because we are making use of the heat transfer vinyl.

- ❖ You'll make use of the circuit weeder tool to get rid of the excess vinyl pieces from your design.
- ❖ Then, you'll arrange the vinyl on top of the clean folded towel. You would have to get that positioning properly because you wouldn't want it aligned to the left more than the right or vice versa.
- ❖ Next, we would cover the towel with another piece of cloth

preferable another tea towel then we would iron it.

- ❖ Once the heat has been able to pass through the fabric successfully, and the vinyl is firmly stuck to the fabric, you should peel away the plastic backing.

- ❖ I placed a cardstock backing right underneath the top layer of the towel, and I used the metallic cloth/fabric paint in champagne, silver, and gold as shown in the picture below to add a little aesthetics in the form of bright dots.

- ❖ Make sure the paint completely dries before you remove what is underneath. And you should do it carefully because you wouldn't want to stain the sides. Natural right?

The Cricut can cut through several materials, leather inclusive so let us about that. The next project idea I would give you is named: DIY Leather Cuff. It is more like a leather cuff bracelet

Items that you need:

- ❖ A small piece of leather. You can get that anywhere you wish to.
- ❖ A silver coated bracelet chain or cording. Any color you want is preferable.
- ❖ Some round nose jewelry pliers. You can also use some regular old needle nose pliers; also, they would work just fine.

- ❖ The Cricut explore which has a deep cut blade
- ❖ Little jump hoops. (optional though)

Steps:

- ❖ You create a design, or you just pick one from your design space. I made use of lace here, and I changed the size, cut it into a paper to have that exact measurement first before I cut the expensive leather. You can't just start with the leather or else you'll end up wasting it.
- ❖ After cutting the leather into the shape I want then I began to assemble the bracelet. Remember I made mention of a silver coated bracelet chain. The picture below should make it all sink.

* After cutting the design, the only thing left is for you to size your chain for that lovely bracelet of yours.
* If you want to do something of this nature, you can add the links into the leather. Never tear the leather to support the links. I don't think that is even possible.

Assembling the bracelet

Final results

This design would look intricate at first
but be sure you practice it with
something else and always visualize the
end result even if it is from the start.
That is what would help you and guide
you.

How to make stickers using Cricut print.

I would share with you how I used a Cricut print and another cut to create that unique ice cream spoons as well as cups in my child's birthday party. I tell you, this is one of the best ways to add color to your party. The designs and themes were just awesome, and I am sure you would also want something similar to that. And why I think you'll love this is because it is simple! There is a lot of beauty in simplicity.

Supplies

- ❖ Cricut Explore Air 2 machine
- ❖ Printable Sticker Paper
- ❖ And Yes, that's all.

Process

- ❖ Like every other process, you log into your Cricut design space, and you start to design. The very good thing about all these designs is that some sites give links to their designs. Yes, you'll just click on it, and you'll have them downloaded on your device. It is that simple

❖ Make sure you start a new project in the Cricut design space. You'll see *images* written on the left side of the screen. Make use of the search bar to get your images. I found ice-cream, and I used it.

❖ Don't just use the images like that; you click *flatten.* You can find this command at the bottom right-hand side of your design space screen. What the flatten button does is that it turns all the parts of the images to one whole piece than a separate cut file.

❖ Reshape each cone by clicking on it. Next, you drag the right part of the box to give that size you want. Each ice-cream was 1" so that they would fit well. You may have multiple rows of ice-cream just like me. You make use of the *select all button* then you press Edit. Another option would pop-up, and that would be *copied.* So you can copy and paste as you do on your computer while using only the Edit button. Make sure you use this tip for copy and paste next time.

❖ You have your design ready for you to print. You click to save the project as usual then you press the *print then cut* button.

❖ Check to see if everything looks fine then press "Continue". Remember that you are making stickers so you'll load it with sticky paper.

❖ After printing, you should adjust the dial on the machine to the correct setting. I prefer to use the Vinyl setting when I am using the thick Cricut paper. You might also want to do the same. Carefully put your sticker paper on the paper cutting mat. Load them into the machine while you simultaneously push it up against the rollers. After that, you press the load/to unload key.

❖ Flashing *Go* button is next. Because of the intricacies of these stickers, you'll probably wait for some minutes.

Let me share a quick tip right here. When you cut design, and you want to cut it once more, you can push the flashing button again without touching the mat or paper. But you should be aware that you can't pull out the mat or even move the paper before you decide to use this method.

I was able to decorate the spoons by peeling off a sticker and sticking it on the end of the spoon. For the ice-cream cups, you need to put on your creative cap. You can decide to line up the ice cream stickers up in a row on the cups or scatter them whichever you choose. Don't let your guest be able to guess your decoration. A surprise is also an act of beauty.

The next craft here would be how to make a personalized pillow with Cricut. Cricut is a fantastic machine. I was able to make a personalized pillow within 15 minutes. And I am sure you can do that. This time around, I didn't make use of your regular explore air, but I used the Cricut maker, and I made the design on my iPhone. Remember that I mentioned to you that you could make use of any gadget you want. What I would be sharing here would be different from the regular thing you've been used to. It is good to explore the variety and enjoy the peculiarity of things because *variety is the spice of life.*

Supplies

- ❖ Cricut Maker or any of your favorite Cricut machine. But the maker is preferred here.
- ❖ Glitter Iron On Vinyl and yes, you're free to choose any vinyl you want.
- ❖ Iron On Protective sheet
- ❖ Your pillow cover as well as insert.
- ❖ Easy Press Mat.

Steps

- ❖ You can start by opening the Cricut design space on your smartphone. Yes, we are using our phones this time around. Make sure you start a "New project" It is there in the home tab.

- ❖ You pick the text icon and get to work. Type what you desire and chose that preferred font. I chose Stewart for this one. Make it larger or smaller depending on how you want it but one thing you should understand is that size matters, and that of your pillow should also be considered.

- ❖ Pick the text icon again, go to the next line and type in a precise Est. year. Make sure it is centralized beneath the last name.

- ❖ Then you pick both text boxes at the same time then press the attach button below. You would see a pop up then you'll click on *actions*. What this would do is that it would attach the two text boxes together making them one so that when cutting it would be centered.

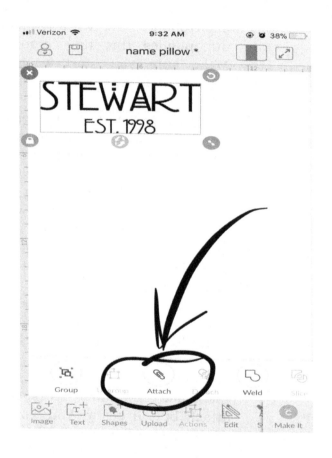

❖ The step that follows requires you to click the *make it* button then the mat screen would appear. At this point, you would want the mirror (for iron-on) to be on

❖ After doing this, the mat would show your image from the back view (the mirrored one) once you're ready to load it on your Iron On Vinyl. You'll make sure that the shiny side of your mat is facing down then you'll press continue.

❖ After the design is cut, you are expected to use a weeder to remove the excess vinyl and make sure your design is centered on your pillow cover.

❖ The next step involves using EasyPress. You would have to set the temperature and timer on the EasyPress for the vinyl as well as the cloth or shirt material.

❖ Use the Iron-on protective sheet to cover your design and place the EasyPress on the protective sheet. Next, you'll press the Cricut button. You can remove it immediately the timer has beeped. You'll hit the backside of your pillow for 10-15 seconds while the pillow cover remains in the flip over the position.

❖ Allow the Iron-on to cool, and you can just simply remove your transfer sheet. Easy right?

We aren't through with leather so I would give you another project idea that requires the use of leather. We would be talking about DIY leather key fob gift idea.

Supplies

❖ Key fab templates
❖ The standard grip cutting mat
❖ Faux leather. Feel free to pick any color. I'll be using brown, silver and beige
❖ Cricut Explore Air 2
❖ Paper crafting set

- ❖ Some Keyrings
- ❖ Rivets
- ❖ The Cricut black pen. This is an optional item.
- ❖ A pebbled Faux leather sampler pack in this project I made use of black and blue colors.
- ❖ Gorilla Glue

Process

- ❖ You know the first process right?. . The design space. You chose your design, and you set the dial to Custom while you chose faux leather. If you're thinking of personalizing your leather Key fob, you can go ahead to load a Cricut pen into that machine. It would look like the image below.

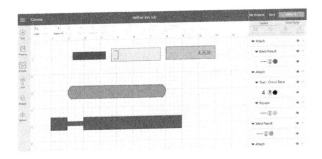

The three templates would look like these after cutting.

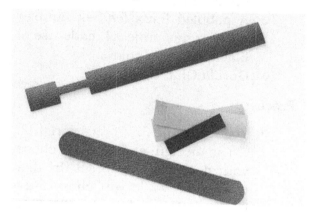

* Next, you'll use the piercer to poke holes for the rivet. You should make sure that the holes are big enough for the rivet base to fit. Remember, it must fit tightly.
* Carefully slide the key ring onto the key fob. The two ends must be parallel to each other. Make sure you push the longer end of the rivet through the leather layers from the back.
* Put the rivet tip over the rivet base then you use a rivet mallet

immediately on top of the rivet. Gently strike because you wouldn't want to spoil the rivet but make sure it is very firm.

❖ I made use of the rubber handle of a hammer to strike because we need that gentle but firm touch. That is the final process. But you can make use of your Cricut pen to personalize it. Write your husband initials on it. However, there are several designs for this project.

❖ The next style would be very different. You would be making use of 3 pieces of faux leather, and you would use a stitch to secure the keychain instead of the rivet.

❖ You'll start from the design space with the template which we have from the first project.

❖ You would insert the small black faux leather piece into a slot in front of the DIY leather Key fob. You would secure both pieces together with some glue. You should make sure to leave it to dry overnight.

❖ Next, you'll make holes marking the positions for stitching with that piercing tool. Then with a large needle plus a black embroidery floss you should begin to start the stitch from the inside so that you can be able to conceal the knot at the back of the key fob.

❖ The needle should be placed through the other hole then you'll slide the key ring, and you stick through on the back once more. You should complete the stitch by going from the front especially from the top of the key fob to the inside.

❖ Next, you would tie the knot and then you'll trim off the excess embroidery floss away. The picture below would help that sink.

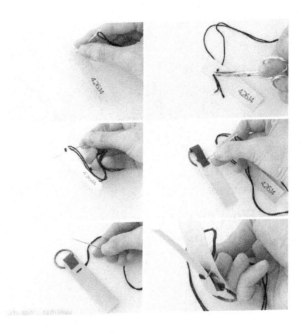

❖ Place some glue between the front and the back of your DIY leather key fob, and you'll hold them together overnight. How? You can use a bobby pin for that.

❖ You can personalize. Names, anniversary date or anything you may want to write. This project is an excellent gift for men.

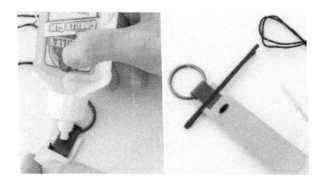

Final product

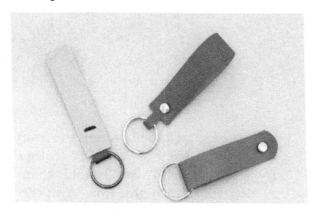

The next project here would be different from what we have been doing. I would like to work on regular conventional designs. This project is *a Pop-up butterfly card* which is good for a Mother's Day celebration, summer birthdays and anyone who loves butterflies.

There are several versions of this card because obviously there are several, countless number of butterflies. However, for all versions, you would need the following items:

- ❖ A 65 Ib. cardstock which should be in the complementary or opposing colors. You should have 1-3 sheets of the wings; a sheet meant for the outside of the card while the other sheet is meant for the inner part.
- ❖ Cricut machine for cutting out your butterfly.
- ❖ Adhesive spray. The 3M spray mount is preferred here.

Process:

- ❖ The first thing here unlike other is that you should cut out your cardstock. And the only way you can do this is to work on it from your design space. Working on a butterfly is not easy. I must confess, but there are over 50,000 patterns, shapes, and objects to guide you into making that perfect shape. The beautiful thing is that you can check online, understand how it is constructed or you download the file online and work on it. Any way you choose, just make sure you have that butterfly ready. Mine was something like this;

After cutting these intricate pieces. They would look so much like the picture below:

I know you're probably thinking, how would I be able to do this? First, you can start with the simple versions. Just get two halves of the butterfly together then you can wrap that outer card all around them. Make sure you make use of an adhesive spray to stick the rectangle sections from the slotted butterflies to that outer card but be careful as you do so because you wouldn't want to get any glue on the wings.

❖ You may be thinking of assembling the fantasy butterfly or something looking more like a monarch butterfly. The first thing you should consider doing is to set the butterfly aside and spray them very well; then they should be an interval of 30 seconds before you move to the next process.

❖ This process requires you to place the inner rectangle sections on those slotted butterfly wings while watching the way you place them in the middle top-to-bottom so that they don't overlap on the body of the beauty.

- ❖ Put the wing color pieces on the butterfly wing. You may decide to choose the fantasy rainbow butterfly you would use one full wing piece.
- ❖ For the monarch butterfly, you would use six butterfly pieces which would all fit in together like that puzzle. Just note the way you place these pieces so that you'll position them well perfectly. Keep covering those areas and do the same for the second wing.

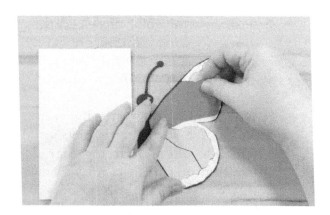

When you have the wing color in place, you should spray the final wing pieces also with the adhesive which you've been using right from time to cover the colored wing. Make sure that you line up the back wing so that it would sync with your pattern.

❖ You'll be required to hold the assembled wings where the body of the butterfly meets the rectangle.
❖ Each part should be slotted together side by side from one side then to the other from top to bottom.
❖ What is followed next? You place that outer card. How can you do this? First, you fold the butterfly and put the small black butterfly cuts you have gotten

from the Cricut back into their positions. Doing this would allow you to protect the inner cardstock especially when the next step comes on.

❖ Protect the wings with some of your scrap paper. I made use of blue scrap paper in the picture below. So you'll spray both the front and back of that your folded piece.

The next process if for you to remove the black butterfly inserts that would show some white butterflies also. Then you would line up the outside card with those pretty looking butterflies so that all the butterflies images are all lined up perfectly.

❖   Place the black and orange butterfly into those empty spaces that are present on the front of the card so that it would cover the adhesive card beneath it.

❖   Don't forget to be creative by adding extra butterfly inserts inside the card also. The most beautiful thing about this is that you can create that 3 D effect by folding the butterfly up a little bit. The process seems to be very complex but trusts me; it's worth your time.

I wouldn't want us to shy away from any project. So the next would be woodwork. It was the fourth of July. So I decided to create a *We the people* farmhouse sign. It was cool because I completed the project in my parent's house and trusted me; they loved it. Wouldn't we like a project made with the use of a Cricut machine?

Supplies:

- ❖ 1″ by 4″ common board which would be cut to 18" by 2
- ❖ 1″ by 2″ common board which would be cut to 18″ by 2
- ❖ 1″ by 2″ common board to be cut to 8.5″ by 2
- ❖ Don't think much about the measurements because when all is said and done, you should have a sign which is 19. 5″ by 8.5″. However, you should make sure that you get at least a good 1″ by 2″ board which could be actually 3/4″ by 1.5″ when you're buying your wood.
- ❖ Nail gun
- ❖ Wood Glue
- ❖ Saw
- ❖ Transfer Tape
- ❖ Some Black Vinyl
- ❖ Cream paint. I made use of Country Chick Vanilla Frosting.

Process:

Before going into the process, there are some things you need to get right. You should get your measurements right. If you don't know how to use a saw or you don't have one, tell the lumber who sold it to you to help you cut it. Make sure you paint it also. I remembered that I did a solid 2 coats allowing it to dry in-between coats and I did stain all the frame pieces.

- ❖ While the paint is drying, you should use your Cricut to explore air 2 to cut the vinyl.
- ❖ I just visited Google and typed in *we the people* I clicked on images, and I saw more than what I needed. I saved it as a .svgfile and uploaded it to the design space. Remember that your design space has several fonts so you might not want to do this.
- ❖ In the design space, you would size the letters into 5" by 16". Make sure they are centralized.
- ❖ Pick up your neatly painted wood. Be sure that it is dry

then you apply that wood glue to its breathes then you would add another piece to it once again. Approximately there would be 3″ apart.

❖ Then you would apply wood glue to the short sides and make sure that all the frame pieces are positioned well. This would build the strength of the sign, and it would make it look very good.

❖ You can also continue by applying wood glue and nails to individual pieces.

❖ Make sure the paint is totally dry before you start to apply your vinyl.

❖ It is advisable that you trim your vinyl properly to just around the letters you need. This would make it very easy for you to work with and you should do the same with your transfer tape.

❖ Stick the vinyl to the wood, press then gently remove the vinyl covering.

"We the People"
Farmhouse Sign

This next project should come as a surprise for you. We are using a Cricut machine to make wedding cards. Wedding cards? *Isn't that too risky?* Not at all. In fact, it is quite easy and simple. And I am sure with this information you would be able to save some money. I know that wedding cards are always expensive. Just imagine each card cost $3 and you are sending 200+ invitations that are a whopping $600 for invitations alone. So we would call these project the

DIY wedding invitations. Making your wedding card would just cost you a little over $40 because that is the amount for the supplies meant for 200+ invitations. You'll be spending $40 instead of $600! We all know that wedding cards are not like your regular cards they would have to carry the theme of the event which includes the color. My favorite is the coral and turquoise combination. After that, you need to choose the wordings of your invitations. The host? The venue? Is the invite meant for both the ceremony and the reception? You should be able to provide answers to these questions. If you have no idea on the wordings, go online, or you probably have one wedding card with you. Make the necessary changes and carve out your own words once you have been able to get all these ready. We can proceed.

Supplies:

- ❖ Cardstock: The cardstock I used here; coral, turquoise and grey.
- ❖ 10″ Paper Doilies
- ❖ Different Cricut Pen but the 4 Fine Tip Black one.
- ❖ Cricut Explore air machine

- ❖ Ribbon, string or twine. The turquoise ribbon is used here.
- ❖ A Turnbow Adhesive Roller. If you can't get that you can use the double-sided tape.

Process:

- ❖ The measurement for the invitations here is 5″ by 8″. The invites were in two different tones. So the first thing to do is to design a rectangle 5″ by 8″ in the design space. Creating a rectangle is quite easy. You click on the *insert shape* button, and you pick the square that you require. Next, you press the lock button so that the length and the width wouldn't be the same. You would have to click on the Edit Tab to change its size to 5″ width and 8″ height.
- ❖ Make use of the duplicate button to make another similar rectangle. I hope you've forgotten the duplicate process.
- ❖ Send the design to the Cricut machine making sure that your dial is on cardstock.

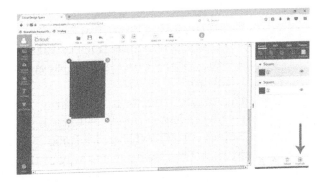

The next process here is quite different from what we've been doing. Notice that most times when we are working on a project we just talk about designing, cutting and then finishing but this time we would have to make part of the designing process on another application. The actual invitation would be in Microsoft Word. It is quite easy. Make sure the ruler is on the screen, and you can make this possible by clicking on the VIEW TAB.

❖ Draw a text box which should measure 7.5″ tall by 4.5″ wide.
❖ Compose your invitation in the text box. Make sure you use the

appropriate fonts and sizes. For this project, I used the Poor Richard and Wilder Fonts.

❖ Make the invitation horizontal by giving the box a 90-degree rotation.

❖ Eliminate the text box line by right-clicking on the text box. Select OUTLINE and chose NO FILL. This would remove the outline of the box. We need the space, not the rectangle.

❖ Remember we have two different colors so you should copy and paste. This would make it two invitations for one page.

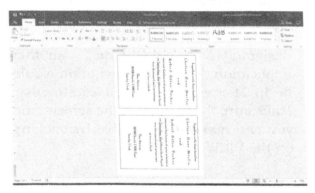

❖ You go back to the Cricut design space, and you'll create an 8.5″ by an 11″ rectangle. You input another rectangle, but that one would be 7.5″ by 4.5″ (that is the same size as your textbox on Microsoft Word)

❖ Duplicate the second rectangle so that there would be two similar rectangles. Place the two smaller rectangles into the bigger ones just close to where the text boxes are in the word document.

❖ Pick all three rectangles by dragging around the largest rectangle and click on ATTACH

❖ Allow the 8.5″ by 11″ rectangle surface by clicking on the eye icon.

❖ Send the design to the Cricut.

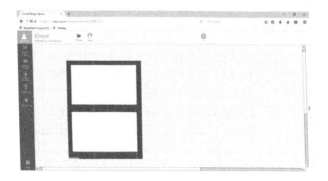

The next process requires you to put invitations together

- ❖ Make use of a Tombow adhesive roller or your double sided tape to apply the teal invitation on that grey backdrop.
- ❖ In the Cricut design space. Create a new page. And add a heart which should be 2″ wide.
- ❖ Type in the bride and groom's initial into the heart. Make sure it is centralized. During this, the initials should be in WRITE not cut.
- ❖ Place a circle above the initials.
- ❖ Blend circle and heart. Blend in the sense that you should put the circle inside the heart, that is where the hole would be.

- ❖ Cut and write hearts.
- ❖ Get a 10″ paper doilie around the invite and fold it.
- ❖ Make use of the ribbon, string or twine to fasten the heart to the invite and tie at the back.

And there you have it. What would have cost you $600 looking at you in the eyes, a product of your own hands, created by you, designed by you all within some minutes? With the help of your, Cricut Air explore cutting machine. Gradually, you're moving from the world of craft to more of visual designs. More also, you've been able to gain new knowledge of how to make use of Microsoft Word, a different app which is totally different from what you've been using.

DIY
Wedding Invitations

I feel we should really talk some more about children project especially with the use of leather. So the next project is DIY with Cricut explore leather bows. This is as simple as the key fob.

Supplies:

- ❖ Leather or Faux Suede. I used the Faux for this project.
- ❖ Cricut Explore
- ❖ Strong Grip Cricut Mat
- ❖ Some Binding Clips
- ❖ French Barrette clips
- ❖ The Bow Cricut Design space file (not necessary because you can always design yours)
- ❖ Transfer Tape
- ❖ E6000 Glue

Process

- ❖ To the Design space! It is a bow. You should know the shape. Design and measure also.
- ❖ Make sure you line your faux suede with the transfer tape. If you're using leather, it is the same process. This process would make the grip of the fabric firm, and it wouldn't leave fuzz all over your mat. You should never stick the fabric on the strong grip mat just like that, you should have something underneath, and that is the transfer tape.
- ❖ Pick the faux leather option on your smart dial. This means that

the Cricut would cut through the material twice especially when your images are just too close to each other, it can catch up with the material and pull the material. You wouldn't want this to happen so there should be flexible space between images. Especially when you're previewing your mat, this would save the material in the long run and definitely save a lot of stress and headaches.

- ❖ You should not be scared of using scissors if there is a knick in the leather.

- ❖ Start with all the pieces stretched out. You might decide to fold the longest piece so that there is a converging point at the middle.

- ❖ Hold that middle with your E6000 glue and a binding clip.

- ❖ You might have made more than one bow what you need right now is to arrange the longer pieces.

- ❖ Apply some glue at the back of the middle position and stick your bow to it. Make sure that you secure that position with a binding clip.

- ❖ Allow it to dry for some minutes before we take the next step
- ❖ Put some of the E6000 on the barrette and place that back piece on it.
- ❖ Apply the glue to that small middle piece of yours. Fold it over the bow at that mid-point till it reaches the back of the barrette.
- ❖ Hold it down again with the binding clip and allow what you have done to dry for some hours before you stick them into your hair so that there wouldn't be any case of a bow sticking to the hair.

Simple huh? You can gift this to your child, and you can also make use of it sometimes. But instead of gifting it to her, both of you should work on it together. Wouldn't that be fun?

The fabric alphabet is the next project. If you're looking for the perfect gift for toddlers and baby showers, the fabric alphabet is a very good way to start. They are super cute, and they are very simple to make also. However, this project is best handled with a Cricut maker. This doesn't mean that a Cricut air can't possibly do its work. Not at all, the Cricut can work pretty good, but the ideal machine to be used here is the Cricut maker. The project has been simplified into three layers. Fabric, quilt batting and then fabric again. The edges seemed raw whenever I stitch them, so I left them raw. It made it have that clean and tender feeling.

Supplies:

- ❖ Fabric.
- ❖ A sewing machine
- ❖ A Cricut Fabric Mat
- ❖ A fabric alphabet cut file which is something you can always work on.
- ❖ Cricut Maker.

Process:

- ❖ The first process is to work on the design. Fine, there are fonts in the program, and I am sure you would like one of them. However, you should learn to edit it. You can work on letterings and words alike. And you might decide to get some by going online. Any choice you make is okay.

- ❖ There would be several letters with different fabrics.
- ❖ If you would be changing fabrics intermittently while you are working you should go into the color sync tab which is on the right hand of the design space; you can move the letters around that way. This is better than for you to change it individually.
- ❖ You can start with cutting off the batting first. I chose to quilt batting from the cut setting, and I placed my batting where it is supposed to be. It is advisable that you cut all the black letters from the batting. In case the batting is messed up, you can just change the color of it, and it would be laced o the mat for recutting.
- ❖ The process next is cutting of fabric. The alphabet is made up of regular and flipped letters. You'll use both. However, there are some letters like "A" which definitely the same from front or back. But when "B" comes into the scene, you'll need a regular B and a backward B.

- While cutting the fabric, I was able to sort them out with batting. I was able to gather all A's to a separate side, all B's to another side, so they were all ready when it was time to sow.
- To create that letter sandwich you would need to place the back of the letter with the right side of the fabric then the batting comes in the middle. While doing this, you should be able to see the right side of the fabric on the front and the back also.
- When it was time to sew, I made use of the edge of the presser foot as a guide. I wanted something less, so I sewed a couple of stitches so close than I continued around the letter. When sewing you should start in the center.
- After stitching, nothing is left.

These letters a great for babies and toddlers as it would help them with learning letters and sounds.

Thanksgiving Favor Box. You might have noticed that I didn't focus on so much on the holiday projects. Cricut project shouldn't be seasonal all the time. The DIY thanksgiving favor boxes like most Cricut projects in this book are easy to make with a little help from the Cricut maker we can get the project done within minutes.

Process:

- ❖ Create the box on the same design space. Study the structure of boxes, draw them out before you start working on the design space.
- ❖ You should make use of the Cricut maker to cut out the box template. It is important that you need to follow the step-by-step instructions in the design space guide.
- ❖ Next, you load the cardstock in. Feel free to pick any color you want and place on the mat into the machine. Also, you'll need pens and scoring stylus which would come in handy when you want to make marks and fold lines.
- ❖ Make sure the paper is left flat instead of curling. Be sure to cut

out all the box templates properly.

❖ A very good trick here when you are doing this kind of project you should turn the mat over and remove the mat from the paper, you should never remove the paper from the mat. It is very risky. This trick has been working well for me, and it has saved countless of project work.

❖ Next, you would fold all along the score lines on the box. Be sure to use your fingernail or a credit card to crease those edges well.

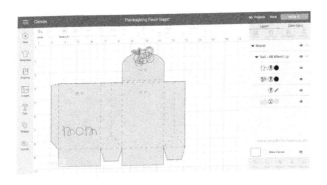

❖ Turn it over and make use of a tape runner or the quick drying glue to make that adhesive line along the line on the right-hand side.

- ❖ Fold box and line up those edges. Gently press the other end and hold it in place till it becomes firm.
- ❖ Fold all flaps which are opened at the bottom of the box. Then you should add that line of adhesive along with the interior of the longer flaps.
- ❖ You should also fold the smaller flaps on each side also.
- ❖ Stand it up, and you can fill it with a lot of treats.

This project is one of my best. I love it because it has to do with the mobile phone. Yes, the phone. Not using the app on the phone but designing and using the Cricut to beautify the phone. Have you ever seen the coating on a regular phone and you wonder *wow, this looks good*? You can use the Cricut machine to make your phones look good. You can give that regular phone a different look. You'll definitely be proud of it.

Having said that, the name of the project is; Cricut personalized phone cases. Unlike the last two projects we talked about, this particular project requires a Cricut Explore. It follows almost the same process which we've been using for a while now. However, the materials used and the process makes it almost impossible to think that the product is homemade or customized. If you are this outgoing type, you'll probably get a lot of *I love this, where did you get it from?* From others. Then you'll be so proud to talk about how you were able to make it all by yourself.

We can create this phone case in a matter of minutes.

Supplies:

- ❖ Transfer Tape
- ❖ A clear phone case
- ❖ Cricut Design Space files or your own regular design.
- ❖ Adhesive foil vinyl or you can also make use of the standard permanent vinyl.

Process:

- ❖ First, you set up a new template on your design space. I am sure you already know how to open a new file by now.

- ❖ If you go through the list of objects, you'll see phone cases and even sizes plus the model.

- ❖ For this project, we would be using the iPhone 6. You can make use of the Android devices also.

- ❖ I also make use of watermelon, pineapple, and cherries also.

- ❖ So, I would get an adhesive foil sheet and my inexpensive clear cases. I have up to six different cases because I enjoy the durability of the rubber. However, I hope the image wouldn't peel off easily because it is a plastic bond.

- ❖ After you might have selected your canvas, you are to get your design, and you paste till there is no space to cover the entire design space. When you are attaching the images, you would want them to cut in the way you've arranged them so that they would print out the way you want them.

- ❖ On your Cricut explore smart dial you chose custom and pick from the available drop-down menu *Cricut Adhesive Foil* or any material you might be using.

- ❖ Make sure after cutting you remove unwanted fills of vinyl and place the transfer tape over your design while pressing the Vinyl over the project.

- ❖ We are aware that the Cricut transfer tape can be very sticky so be very careful when using it. And that is why we also make use of adhesive foil because the foil is very sturdy. You may be making use of the permanent vinyl. That is good because it is light and it would definitely not ruin the surface or the vinyl which you're using.

- ❖ It is also nice if you can be able to use grid lines on the Transfer Tape.

- ❖ Next, you peel out the transfer tape up which would have your images imprinted on it then place it on the desired object which is your phone case. Make sure those images have a good press so that when you're lifting the transfer tape, the image would still remain intact.

Conclusion

I am sure you've been able to gain a lot from this book. One key thing you should have is that hunger for more, and I am sure I have been able to create that hunger thereby showing you amazing thing the Cricut machine can do when you use it.

Creativity is endless; the uses of the Cricut machine are endless. I am sure you're fired up. I'll advise you to learn more, take on projects that are challenging they make you better. Practice breeds perfection. Happy Cricuting! Lol.

Feel free to contact me if you have questions. Thank you.

Thanks again for taking the time to download "The Ultimate Cricut Guide for Beginners" book!

You should now have a good understanding of what is Cricut machine, what are the uses of it, what kind of supplies you'll need to use it, all about Explore Air 2, Design Space and lots and lots of project ideas you can create by yourself!

If you enjoyed this book, please take the time to leave me a review on Amazon. I appreciate your honest feedback, and it really helps me to continue producing high quality books.